Hunting Somerset Dragons

Some local lore for the more discerning pagan...

By
Roy Adams

ACKNOWLEDGEMENTS

Our thanks for their support in this work to Rosmerta, the Lord and Lady at Dundon, the Water Mother at Ninesprings, Sul under Bath and, of course, Camulos and Epona, the tutelary powers of my own land. Thanks also to my human helpers and guides:-

Harry

Lesley

Colin & Carol

Pauline & Alan

Yuri & Claudine

R.J.

Celia

Anthony

and Nigel our intrepid charioteer

and others too numerous to list here!

CONTENTS

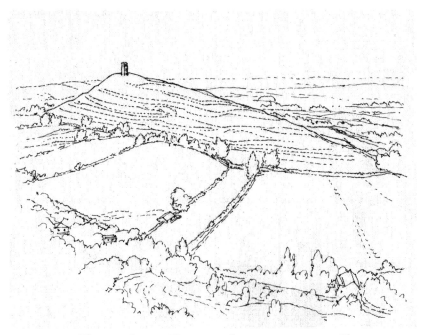

Glastonbury Tor, to show serpent coils

INTRODUCTION

Dragons were a significant part of the material I learned in Essex and I was intrigued, when I moved down here in the '90s, to find that they figured strongly in Somerset lore as well. In fact it was dragon lore that brought Glastonbury to my attention in the first place.

Circa 1970, in the wake of the first Glastonbury festival, a friend showed me a photo of the Tor and we both remarked that it was an obvious dragon hill. A dragon hill sits at the centre of a sacred landscape and tends to have a pole or other axis marker at its top and some representation of the presence of a great serpent coiled around its slopes. The Tor clearly has both features. I didn't know at the time that there was a town called Glastonbury at its foot but a few visits soon clarified that matter

My relationship with the area developed slowly and intermittently through the 70s and 80s, linking threads of Somerset and Essex magic, until, finally, in the mid-90s, I moved to somerset to get married and we have been exploring the Tor's associated sacred landscape ever since.

LOCAL DRAGONS, A SUMMARY

It didn't take me long to root out the main local dragon legends. There are six or seven dragon legends over somerset as a whole but I'm going to bias the evidence by concentrating on our local ones. These are focussed on the villages of Aller and Dinder; the first near the River Parrett not far from Langport and the second in the steep little valley of the River Sheppey near Wells.

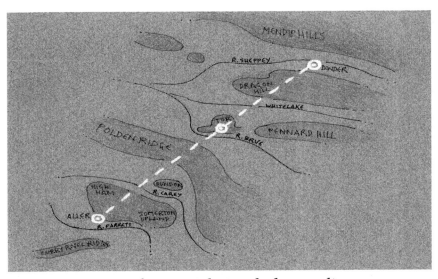

map of area with rough dragon line

I was amused to note that you can draw a pretty good straight line between Aller, Glastonbury Tor and Worminster Sleight; the hilltop, near Dinder, the dragon was supposedly based on. This little hint of structure reminded me of a wonderfully obscure quote from Robert Graves' epic, *The White Goddess*, in which he

6

describes two covens, at South Brewham and Wincanton, and notes that they are both 14 miles from Glastonbury, *'the religious centre for the mainly Brythonic local population'.* This, in turn, prompted me to look more carefully at the local dragon-lore to see if I could pick up any 'old magic' references therein.

In the spirit of true scientific enquiry we paid a visit to the dragon sites at Aller and Dinder in order to get a feel for the spirit of place and the actual layout of both areas. Some things can be gleaned from maps beforehand, however. In both cases the dragon is said to have flown from high land to the south of a river to high land to its north, for example, which may be a graphic way to speak of a crossing between worlds. Consider the old image of the crossing of the river Styx. The south, too, can be read as the realm of the circling sun (i.e. time) while the north is the timeless precinct of the polar stars. At Dinder, both southern and northern locations are accessible on foot and the river-crossing is relatively easy.

However, enough speculation for a moment.. here's what we found on the land.

ALLER, STORY AND VISITS

Story first..

Lets start to the southwest of Glastonbury with the Aller wyrm. This beast lived (in one version of the legend) in a cave in the hillside above the little village of Aller, set on the edge of the levels looking out towards the River Parrett and the long ridge of Curry Rivel to the south and west. The dragon, having made a nuisance of itself by eating livestock and causing general mayhem, was tackled by one John of Aller (either knight or peasant, depending on who you ask, though his 13th century effigy is said to be inside Aller church, against the wall to the right of the entry door) who protected himself with a coating of pitch and a breathing mask and speared the creature up on South Hill. There is said to be an area of bare ground where its blood poisoned the soil. Indeed, you can see such an area on the hillside from the churchyard. There are different endings to the tale as well; in one our John succumbs to the wyrm's breath while in the other he survives to kill the dragon's brood in its cave, conveniently blocking same so it can no longer be found.

John of Aller's effigy?

There are interesting threads leading out of this story; the spear, for instance, still exists and hangs in a wee chapel nearby, also the detail of John's coat of pitch etc. strongly suggests the medieval "plague doctors"who wore just such protection when going their rounds. The village takes the wyrm as its mascot and has a yearly custom of burning large effigies on a public bonfire (including one of the dragon some years back). It also possesses a fine early font (Norman, but said to be Saxon) and may well be the place where Alfred forced Guthrum to be baptised into the christian faith. The little hill the church sits on was once the site of the settlement, the village only moving to its present location after the Glaston monks drained the levels, thus rendering the little island indefensible. The dragon is, of course, a well known pagan symbol, important to both Norman and Saxon in different ways. It was also the term used in post-Roman times for a powerful war-leader (a pendragon was the next rank up) and it is possible that tales of dragons may refer to such folk and their exploits. We will come upon another layer to this idea later..

Now the visit...

Aller is a pleasant little village sat astride the main road from Langport to Taunton at the southwest corner of the area of high land Somerton sits on. Its northeastern part extends up the hillside and is accessed via a partially car-friendly lane which weaves around several sizeable houses and their sloping gardens. The upper part of the lane is really only passable on foot and has a stony little run-off stream trickling down its centre. At the top of this you have a choice of a stile leading to an open field (with a fine view south over the Parrett valley to Curry Rivel, where the dragon is said to have flown from) or a wet track through the woods heading north. The south-facing field is likely the most relevant location for anyone seeking to contact the spirit in the land which the dragon may represent, plus a good place to check out any sunrise/set alignments or horizon markers that may prove relevant... The Pynsent Monument and Curry Rivel church tower might fit in the latter category but one mustn't be blind to prominent natural features... The fact the dragon was speared can be read as a hint that a harmonisation of sky and land energies was intended here. Indeed, the fact that the actual spear is kept nearby, and was once in the tower of Aller church, may hint that the re-enactment of such a linking of worlds is not unknown...

Aller church from south hill top.. centre of picture amidst trees!

Fire and water,

This brings to mind the 12th century Mabinogion and its tale of Arianrhod's curious twins, Lleu and Dylan... the former a variant of Lugh and the latter a sea-god killed by a smith, a specialist in the transformation of the metals (= planets) in the land (= body/soul)... The smith is a lord of fire and Aller, on balance, seems to be a fire location.

Fire can be read as an image of spirit ascending out of its attachment to matter and water as an image of spirit's descent into material expression... reality becoming metaphor over time.

But enough of Aller for the moment. Dinder next. Dinder can be read in pidgin welsh as Din Dwr, meaning "water fort". Water as opposed to Aller's fire perhaps? Sadly this is not its meaning as given in the village's local history, which translates as "house in the valley"... mind you, on thinking about it, these are not so different after all.

DINDER, STORY AND VISITS

Story first..

At Dinder we also start with a wyrm terrorising locals, mainly in the three villages of Dinder, Dulcote and North Wooton, the first two set along the northern side of the valley of the flood-prone little River Sheppey and the third to the southwest of Worminster, but in this case they ask Bishop Jocelyn of Wells to come and deal with it. He cheerfully does so, bringing along his men-at-arms but leaving them behind at the last furlong and carrying on alone to confront and behead the beast. The head he brings back from the fight is said to have been that of a woman, oddly enough, and a custom was instituted that the slaying should be re-enacted every 50 years by a "left-handed man of the cloth" to prevent the dragon returning!

Now Jocelyn was an historic person (circa 1250's) and the story is said to have come from "*illuminated manuscripts at Eton saved from dissolved Somerset monasteries*" so it is at least 16th century in origin. A little more probing here discloses the fact that the earliest version of the tale is in Ranulph Higden's "*Polychronicon*". Higden was a monk in Chester and died circa 1364, his manuscript being stored at Witham Friary near Frome until it was moved to Eton college. The hill of Worminster Sleight, a little south east of

Dinder and across the river, which was the dragon's base, has a Saxon name which means, sadly, "moor church valley" or "true guardians' valley", neither of which helps much in placing the story in a pre-Norman context! There are, however, Norman period images of human headed dragons (always female!) which symbolise the serpent who tempted Eve in that first of gardens in the Torah... Could our dragon be some local Saxon would-be pendragon or even a bit of serpent-cult activity in the deer-park that the local bishop felt obliged to deal with?

And visits...

A preliminary trip to Dinder showed us that it is an estate village serving Dinder House, an imposing residence beside which the church stands. The church is not so ancient but it retains a Norman double-headed dragon atop a south-facing window...

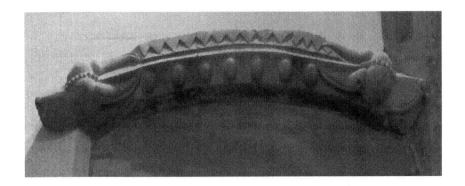

... whose stained glass portrays the dragon-slaying...

… Archangel Michael.

And a bronze effigy of Michael in the southwest corner continues the theme...

… and a nice little dragon-slaying angel, with wings and Norman-ish armour stands in a wee niche above the south porch outer door.

Worminster Sleight, the dragon's lair, is hidden from sight behind the wooded ridge running south of the Sheppey but a steep walk over this ridge takes you to the muddy red soil of the footpath which climbs the sleight, from the top of which fine views may be seen! The footpath is not as accessible as the O.S. map might suggest as the farmer uses the hill as cattle pasture but the climb is worth the red mud and the risk of ticks as the panorama includes the Tor, Worminster Down (known as dragon hill by the travellers who used to live up there), Dulcote Quarry and (if you know just where to look) the Maesbury Hillfort atop the Mendips to the northeast. The beautiful little valley of the Redlake stream heads roughly Tor-wards to the southwest, out into the Hartlake Moor where it joins up with the Whitelake stream out of Pilton's valley, home of the infamous festival at Worthy Farm!

Worminster Sleight hilltop.

Worminster itself, a hamlet made up mostly of a couple of big farms, is said to have a fine cross (we found a modern timber structure atop a stone and concrete blockhouse on the peak of Worminster Sleight, but didn't see one in the hamlet below) and remnants of an ancient chapel (which we didn't find either, this requires further visits to check and clarify).

An intriguing bit of local colour in Dinder is the sign hanging "outside the beer retailer's house" which shows the crest of the Somerville family, a blue wyvern standing atop a twelve-spoked wheel! Blue for water? 12 spokes for a zodiac? More research needed there, too, I think...

Dinder's dragon sign

The last re-enactment was supposed to be in 2001 but was postponed for a year due to a Foot and Mouth outbreak (did the dragon sneak back in that year?) A rather fine children's mosaic commemorates it just beyond the Bishop's Palace gardens in Wells.

In fact, there is also a mosaic of their dragon in Aller, made by a local potter. Well worth a visit!

ANALYSES OF SITES AND LORE

This leads us into looking at the general context of our tales, the history and landscape they are set in...

The alignment I noticed earlier between Aller and Worminster and the Tor turns out to develop interesting features when checked out more carefully. The precise line runs between Aller church, the Tor top and Maesbury Hillfort. Worminster Sleight is a little east of the line, which crosses Worminster Down roughly where a steep, spring-fed stream emerges amidst hilltop woodland. Now, seen from Maesbury fort the Tor stands at the midwinter sunset point with reasonable accuracy. The same can't be said of the Tor-Aller alignment as the two are not intervisible but the top of the high land west of Somerton can be seen and the midwinter sunset line seen from Aller has the sun dropping amidst some intriguing old villages set at the west end of the Curry Rivel ridge... more research is needed here too! Of course, if you look the other way along our alignment you get to watch the midsummer sun climbing up out of the land and we don't know which direction was relevant. Knowing the time of year of each dragonslaying would help here...

Our line takes us through three major river basins; the Brue (and its tributaries the Sheppey, Redlake and Whitelake), the Cary and the Parret. Given the tendency of local tribal groups to identify with the river basins they lived in our line might suggest some sort of intergroup cooperation... a druid system linking Lugus-connected tribal assembly places might be an idea worth expanding further... Glastonbury, at least, has all the features required of such a ritual assembly site. The general pattern of Lughnasa rites required a "Lugus hill", suitable springs, a shrine for the old provider-god Lugus comes to trick (out of his harvest wealth) and a pen for the sacred bulls slain for the rites (Taurus rose in the east at lughnasa in the bronze age, when these rites were devised). Another common component of these rites was the interaction of a warrior hero with a chthonic dragon (Hydra rises after Taurus..). More on this in the next section! Does this all begin to sound familiar? Our 13th century dragonslaying Normans are not so far from such a scenario... do we have any interesting Lughnasa sunrise or sunset alignments from Aller or Worminster?

Lugus and fiery spear

Now let us jump forward to the 1700s, when William Stukely writes of *'some saint or other'* clearing the area between the Tor, Ham Hill and Cadbury Castle of serpents. Certainly there are many dragons cut into church walls in the area not cleared of serpents; consider those in Somerton church...

... and the intriguing works in Stoke sub Hamdon church... not only a warrior-dragon fight above a tiny northern window...

… but a bigger stone above a north door showing the three fire-signs as visible around spring equinox midnight!

In both of the latter the stone carvings seem to speak of the arch of the sky and the Milky Way, ancient road of souls to and from the timeless source-spring at the Pole... Link this to the parallelogram formed by these sites and Burrow Mump (hinted at by Katharine Maltwood and described in detail by John Michell) and to Robert Graves' 14 mile circle of witch covens around the Tor and we get a distinct hint of some sort of pagan ideology continuing in the region...

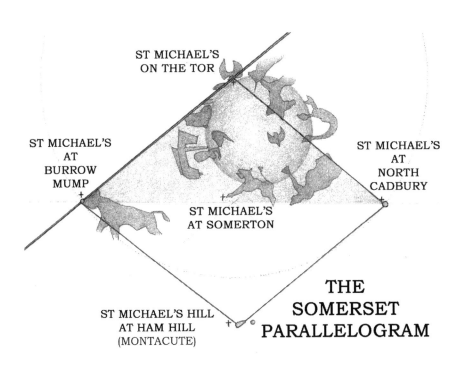

ST MICHAEL'S
ON THE TOR

ST MICHAEL'S
AT
BURROW
MUMP

ST MICHAEL'S
AT SOMERTON

ST MICHAEL'S
AT
NORTH
CADBURY

ST MICHAEL'S HILL
AT HAM HILL
(MONTACUTE)

**THE
SOMERSET
PARALLELOGRAM**

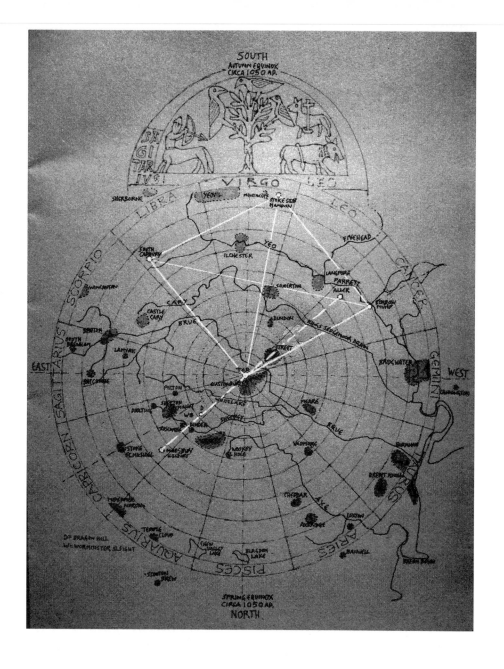

the stoke - sub- hamdon carvings overlaid on a rough map showing the parallelogram and dragon-free triangle, and a hint of a big zodiac!

OLDER NOTIONS OF DRAGONS

Some background, now, to the whole idea of dragons... Serpent images turn up in what is probably religious art from way before the invention of writing. They can be found, in terrestrial and celestial guises, in Sumerian, Babylonian and Egyptian contexts and their meanings are complex and multi-layered even then, if the contemporary stories are to be believed. Consider the horned and four-limbed Mushusshu serpents who guarded gateways and the slaying by Marduk of the celestial dragon Tiamat, whose body seems to have constituted an early zodiac rendered obsolete by precession. Another view of this well worth perusing is that expressed in feminist works such as *"Dragontime"* by Luisa Francia or *"Blood, Bread and Roses"* by Judy Grahn... I'll say nothing of this, consider it homework! Our own wyrms, however, are more likely to resonate with classical European than ancient Middle Eastern imagery, so let's take a peek at these sources.

Greco-Roman first, as much later stuff evolves out of that milieu... Greek culture is a fusion of Egyptian, Minoan and Phoenician ideas with Indo-European notions brought in via migrating tribes from around the Danube. There are underworld serpents, like the Python slain by Apollo on his takeover of the Delphic Oracle, a powerful case of a more general image of serpents as symbols or messengers of ancestors in the land, and water serpents like the Hydra slain by Heracles or the sea monster

Perseus saved Andromeda from (probably the Hydra constellation and the Milky Way respectively). This linking of watery and celestial powers recurs often, hinting at the idea of stars reflected in the underworld and the idea of the cycle of time as a great Serpent Goddess (later a god personifying the year's sacrifices and the sacred Soma, so essential then to the conscious, ceremonial linking of the worlds, which was a fundamental function of religion). See the later section on theory and practise for more detail on how to work with this today... The serpent as ancestor in the land is prominent in Roman lore, based on the Etruscan roots of that lore. Consider the ubiquitous roman Lararium, the domestic shrine to the gods of plenty and the serpentine clan ancestors in the land below.

Roman lararium with land serpent

This shrine was a remnant of an old Roman cult from the time when the people were hill shepherds and had not been influenced by Greek ideas of human-formed divinities... An interesting commentary upon this worldview is found in Radomir Ristic's book on *Balkan Witchcraft*. He speaks of dragons, able to take on human form, who seek out witches as lovers. The children of such liaisons became heroes with great strength and superior powers, having a human material body and a dragon-shaped astral body. Pendragons indeed! An aspect of this sort of idea seems to be present in the Roman military custom of using dragon pennants, though I believe this was a cavalry related practise and most roman cavalry were recruited from conquered peoples who may have brought the custom with them. In Dacia (now Romania) a standard made up of a dragon pennant with a dog's head was quite common (any connection with the dog and snake who lap the blood of the bull sacrificed by Mithras here?) and Dacia was an important Roman province for some time...

*Dacian and Roman dragon-dog standards,plus Bianchini
Tablet with polar draco at centre*

We should also note in passing the Gaulish and British image of the Jupiter Column, developed under Roman rule, in which a rider-god's horse treads down a serpent-legged "Titan" at the top of an oak-decorated world-axis column.

Top of a Jupiter column

Serpents as powers of the below once more; matter mastered by spirit? The circuit of time by the timeless axis? Another stream of relevance here is what is known about the old festival of Lughnasa wherein the trickster-god Lugh, archetype of human sovereignty and intelligence, fools the old chthonic/weather lord into releasing the grain and cattle needful for his human subjects. A part of the festival pattern involved a warrior aspect of Lugh defeating a dragon whose name might mean either "blight" or "fireball/thunderbolt". This serpent is perhaps combined with the old land-god as the snake-legged figure in the Jupiter Column, a Romano-Greek style "Titan" in place of the more native serpent-legged Cernunnos. There exists a fascinating variant of this idea in which Conall Cernach battles a hillfort-defending serpent which darts into his belt and enables him to instantly defeat the fortress and capture its treasures. Here we have an allegory or mystery, a teaching story, in which an outer situation is shown to mirror an inner pattern which, once the leap of understanding has been made, makes available the treasures hidden in the deeper self. The world axis becomes the spine and the serpent moves from the ditch-maze around the upperworld fortress to the protective girdle about the waist. Macrocosm becomes microcosm...

From Romano-Celtic lore to Saxon lore now; not such a huge jump as Saxons served as auxiliaries in the Roman armies for centuries. Saxon dragons tend to be brooding and dangerous powers connected with caves and burial mounds who hoard treasure. Elements here of dragons as war-leaders mingled with dragons as jealous ancestors whose wealth, be it material or spiritual, must be liberated by some courageous clan hero for his people (the Lughnasa pattern above dimly remembered?). Consider the fight of Beowulf and the dragon here... This unholy marriage of war-leader and powerful chthonic ancestor probably underlies the common use of serpents in wargear decoration and formal runescripts!

Such patterns are continued and expanded by the later Vikings and both folk-currents continue as a culture of symbolism when both peoples are Christianised, the older hero-gods being replaced carefully by saints who best fit the local stories and rites...

Quite likely much of the bizarre sculptured symbolism in Saxon and Norman churches; plus the Welsh lake-fairies who act as as sources of culture; the beheaded saints from whose skulls pilgrims drank blessings at holy wells; and the enigmatic well maidens and their guardian knights so common in our Sufi-inspired Grail Romances are all expansions of the old lore in which a would-be ruler must seek to 'marry' the otherworld sovereignty, or ruling archetype, of the land!

WORKING WITH DRAGONS

Theory and practise

Earlier I said I would talk of how dragon lore can be put into practise... Here are a few musings on the matter...

In the bits of lore I was given back in central Essex I found references to "Dragon Lines" which snake about under the land and which provide favourable magical working locations where they cross; Compare the Michael and Mary lines in Broadhurst and Miller's *"Sun and the Serpent"*. There were also considered to be links to the four (or five?) elements which gave a variety of different possible qualities to each crossing. These Dragon Lines also relate to springs and surface rivers so I have come, over time, to see them as flows of different qualities of "fire" in the ubiquitous "waters" within the land.

Please note that "fire" can mean that which generates "light", or consciousness, and "waters" can mean the fluid, ever-changing medium of the imaginal worlds within, which includes our perceptions of the consensus reality we appear to inhabit while awake!

Axis and rim

How does this relate to dragons? Try this... the axis is the timeless centre, heart, of all that is expressed. The rim is the sequence of expression in time. The whole structure, both heart and periphery, is considered a single living being and the serpentine "rivers" are thought of as that being's blood vessels and nerves. This "person in the land" is a reflection of the ancient "person in the stars" who embodies the year (and greater cycles of time by analogy).

The dragons, then, can serve to put us in touch with both the macrocosm and our own inner reflection of the stars, the microcosm.

The stone bowl

A useful form in this context, both as imaginal construct and as physical working tool, is a stone bowl, full of water, which can reflect the light of the stars. It is a model of the system described above and can also be used for various types of scrying or for the connection of awareness to the influence of any particular star of the Zodiac. Mirrors are important traditional gateways connecting inner and outer realms. They can also stand for the nature and function of the awareness looking into them.

An interesting use of such symbolism is the "stone head in the well", the head of the old land-god which is taken out at Lughnasa to be set atop his "holy hill" to overlook the land he empowers.

The stone itself can serve as well in this work. A standing stone, cliff face, cave wall or even a house wall can be used, by an act of "feeling into" the spaces "behind" its solidity, as a way to contact the inner aspect of the land and the presences therein.

To a large extent it is meaningful to see these presences as "ancestors merged with the land" but please don't expect them all to look like us! Just as we have bodies made of matter which obey matter's rules so our forebears now have bodies made of the "substances" of the imaginal realms which obey the deeply unfamiliar rules of those spaces. The nature of dream, and of the inner "place" out of which dream images arise, gives us a few clues.

Sacred landscape

A sacred site is a location set up to make an inner and outer space resonate usefully with each other. Such a site allows easy communion between beings in the inner worlds and those of us still "in the eggshell" of the outer world we grow up in. The purpose of such contact is the mediation and unfolding of divine qualities in conscious practise but, of course, such gates are sometimes misused... Perhaps we should look at some helpful ways to work with such sites.

Walking the land

You and the land have to meet before you can get to know each other. The best place to begin this process is in areas which have the least signs of human overlays; wild woods, moorland, dunes, saltmarsh, rocky outcrops etc. Just go there and be respectful and take careful notice of what you feel and what ideas arise in head and heart. To demonstrate your seriousness try taking a pen and notebook along to record what comes. Also, if you take lunch with you, share it with the land consciously and leave a little for the nonhuman locals. Such exchanges and gifts develop over time in ways personal to yourself and the place, it is impossible to predict what will grow between you but I do advise that you stick to the maxim "do no harm"... Once you have several such contacts in process you can try the same methods in areas with more human overlay, such as agricultural land, parks and gardens. With practice you will learn to navigate between the overlaid human concepts to the "inner light of the earth" beyond and to bring some harmony to the interactions between both layers. Your lunch break in the park can take on depths you would never have imagined!

Some times and tools

Having seen the nature of contact you might want, or might have been asked by the land, to develop the process more systematically. This is where such things as the "wheel of the year" and "circles" and "working tools" can become relevant. This can help to develop precision and purity of exchange with inner contacts, and their innerworld spaces, by using outer symbols resonant with their inherent qualities, a useful thing!

However, there is always the niggly little inner voice that whispers "aren't I a clever magician to be doing all this cool stuff!"... a little inner voice that is always there, but which is fatal to all your efforts if you begin to take it seriously...

But back to times and tools.

The Wheel of the Year is not ancient, it is a Wiccan concept from the 1950's, but that doesn't make it any less valuable as a set of ways to attune with the qualities of the seasonal transitions, both in the land and in yourselves.

Also useful are the change-points of the daily cycle; dawn, noon, dusk and midnight.. the "witching hour" (actually from midnight to 1p.m...).

These "wheels" are but two versions of the idea of the gradual revelation of the qualities of being, much as the sun highlights different aspects of day or year by its leisurely motions (though of course it is actually we who are moving). A visible "enactment" of the slow unveiling of the light of awareness through the course of a life.

A magical circle, with its quarter and cross-quarter points, is a good model of this and motions or orientations in such a circle form a language useful in such an inner/outer meeting place. Much of this has developed over time out of watching and working with the horizon's interaction with the turning heavens, but that is another whole book in itself. The most important part of any circle, however, is the central axis it turns about... the Pole-Star in heavenly terms, the spinal column in bodily terms and the Heart in terms of consciousness. In terms of the land it is simply wherever you happen to be!

Folk speak of "opening and closing the directions" in the context of circle work but you hardly ever see anyone mention "opening and closing the centre"; the Heart, however, is where all directions lead and where all real work happens. The still point of being between polar opposites...

The Mithraic lionhead's heart and hands with keys and thunderbolt

Tools, then... a rod is the axis, a cup is where memories of the watery changes of the rim are collected and synthesised, a platter is the rim process as a whole, a stone is simply where you are now and the hole in its centre is the Heart's "Door into Summer" (to steal a nice old spiritualist metaphor). A knife, so important in the newer magics, is the opener of liminal spaces and the liberator of the life within them.. a cleaned-up conceptual summary of its ancient role in sacrifice. "The blood is the life" as the Torah says...

In my own work I have found that a rod and a stone and a pen and a sketchbook seem to serve well enough in most work.

And back to dragons..

In an old Roman house, as previously mentioned, you would have found a household shrine at which offerings were made to the "gods" of the family, the Lares and Penates. These were basically the spirits of clan ancestors and the heavenly and earthly powers whose qualities shone up out of the land, through them, for the aid and protection of the still-living. Beneath the conventional pictures of the Lares, as young men, lay a great Earth-Serpent. This is the dragon in the land which even now performs these same functions if only it is met and heeded.

A Lararium in your living space would be a respectful touch, even nowadays, but the real meeting place with these powers is the land you sit or stand on at this very moment. You have only to feel down into it and to listen...

Raising the serpent !

Dragon-men...

Radomir Ristic says some interesting things about dragons in his book on *Balkan Traditional Witchcraft*. If the dragon is read as the life-fires moving within the land and their human partner(s) seen as empowered and guided thereby then we reach the interpretation of the subject I was taught in Essex... Consider also the knight who spears the dragon at his feet not as a slayer but as one who consciously unites in himself the timeless spirit-fire of the vertical axis and the ever moving serpent energy in the waters of time.

The purpose of human life, in these terms, is to recognise the dragon-fires within the "waters" of this sensory world and to follow the thread of such "fire", the Path of Detachment, to its source in the heavens at the Heart of being... not an easy task and the subject of many esoteric sagas of the past.

Images to expand and connect.

Conceptual images such as these are well worth studying and meditating upon in our context. If you can devise a way to act them out this connects all three worlds and is even better... You will be surprised by what arises within you if you do the work!

The image of the stars of Draco reflected in dark waters in a stone bowl at midnight... the stars within the land as well as mind within body.

The macrocosm as a projection of the microcosm, radiating out from the heart... the otherworlds are within this one, accessed via the Heart!

Witch-queens...

As mediators of this land-dragon energy/awareness and thus sovereignty-givers to local male rulers, making them "dragons" or "pendragons" if warleaders.

Such contact with the stellar "fire" in the land is equivalent to contact with both "faery" and with "ancestors". It is also relevant within the body/self... This web of themes is present in old tales such as the

Arthurian mythos (Guinevere and the Well-Maidens...) and the likes of Perseus' legend (Andromeda and her sea monster, and snaky-haired Medusa), or the story of Melusine (her serpentine form in the bath), or the tale of Heracles slaying the Hydra serpent and burning off its heads... all of these contain details which can be unfolded to shed useful light.

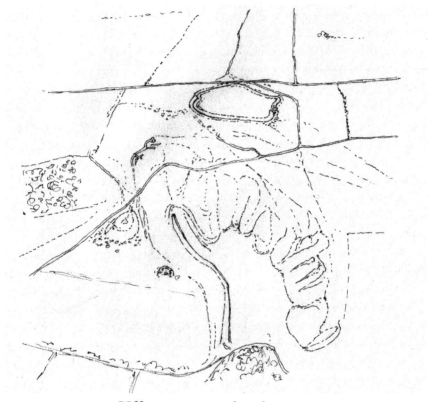

Uffington complex from air

Dragon-riding also... the human practitioner is either riding the dragon-currents of awareness through the land or training the "reptilian brain" to empower inner work such as shamanic "flight"; or perhaps both at once!

Finding places where strong dragon currents cross and summoning them up to empower your visions fits nicely into this scenario. The Old Witch Goddess and God also make sense as the personified awareness of these wild and innerworld realms, be they projected into the physical countryside or sought among the forests of the soul! Consider such places as Uffington, the great bronze-age horse-dragon with Dragon Hill at its base, the great communal meeting enclosure before its face and the spring in the valley below, as a location for whole tribes to participate in such symbolic meetings of worlds. Here underworld and heavens, senses and spirit are called to become one in a location expressive of the divine pattern common to them all.

From the above, we can see new readings of, for example, the woman-headed dragons in church lore which are said to symbolise the "Serpent in Eden", the goddesses of springs and rivers and river-basins and pools and bogs, the ancestor-serpents portrayed in Roman Lararia, even the ancient astronomical fable of Marduk's tiff with Tiamat!

If you read the stone bowl as the land and the waters in it as all waters below the earth then the offering of treasures into bogs, gifts for the star-souls of the ancestors reflected below, a gift calling forth a gift, makes clear symbolic sense.

LIVING DRAGONS

The dragon procession in town

Bringing this all up-to-date, the community of Glastonbury recently celebrated Beltaine with a series of events including mummer's plays, ritual, maypole dancing and processions. Numerous diverse groups wove threads together to make this happen and one of the more colourful features was an encounter between the local red and white dragons!

These beasts, on one level, represented the Red and White Springs below the Tor and the Redlake and Whitelake rivers out on the levels to the north of the town. They are also a reference to the fighting dragons mentioned in the *"Lludd and Llevelys"* tale in the *Mabinogion* and in the story of the young Myrddin Emrys at Vortigern's tower (read them and you will see connections!)

Entrance to King Arthur's Court, Chalice Well

The link to the Red and White Springs was made overt when the dragons passed between these sources in Wellhouse Lane, on their way up to the maypole rites at the top of Bushey Coombe. The red waters are generally seen as female and the white as male (for reasons I shouldn't need to explain) and this links interestingly to their correlations with the numina of conflicting Welsh and Saxon cultures in the Vortigern's tower story... They may also be read as levels of inner work; the King Arthur's Court/White Spring level must be attained before the Blood Spring Goddess may be meaningfully approached!

Red and White are also indicators that something otherworldly is occurring in a myth or hero-tale; a complex field which I'll leave you to explore for yourself in, for instance, old Irish stories.

Just as the acting out of mythic archetypes can have a transformative effect on an individual so can the enactment of mythic rites have spiritually enhancing effects on a community, consolidating its numen and, by the "nearness is likeness" formula, bringing it closer to the powers behind the manifest world.

As you can see from the pictures, the spirit of the dragons is by no means dead!

Glastonbury Dragons in ceremony

BIBLIOGRAPHY

Balkan Traditional Witchcraft- Radomir Ristic

Somerset Dragons- Brian Wright

Parish Church leaflets:-

from Aller...

   King Alfred in Aller,

   the Church

from Dinder...

   Discover Somerset Churches map 2, - Diocese of Bath & Wells

Sadducissimus Triumphatus, referred to in The White Goddess- Robert Graves- p.194-195... note that the 14 mile circle around Glaston is not found in the above. The idea probably came to Graves from some somerset witches of his acquaintance, see his 1960's compilation 'the crane bag'.

Polychronicon- Ranulph Higden

The Mabinogion

Dragontime – Luisa Francia

Blood Bread and Roses – Judy Grahn

ROY ADAMS

Roy grew up in northern Essex when rural villages were still thriving and diverse communities, and the surviving echoes of pagan religion were still lived every day a little behind the scenes... since the 1990's he has lived in Somerset, a refugee from the remorseless spread of London-based materialism!

Printed in Great Britain
by Amazon